The Postman is Late Again

or Help to Get That Job

by
Howard Coates

authorHOUSE®

AuthorHouse™ UK Ltd.
500 Avebury Boulevard
Central Milton Keynes, MK9 2BE
www.authorhouse.co.uk
Phone: 08001974150

First published by AuthorHouse 15/4/2008

ISBN: 978-1-4343-4915-6 (sc)

Printed in the United States of America
Bloomington, Indiana

This book is printed on acid-free paper.

Dedication

I dedicate this book to those who don't give up.
To those who take control of their lives and make no
excuses.
To those who find a way to achieve their goal no matter
what difficulties they may meet.

Contents

The Postman is Late Again!

I didn't see it. I was on top of the bloomin' thing before I realised. 'Great.' Now not only did I have to worry about not having a job, but I'd probably just got a speeding ticket.

It was just after lunch on a sunny Friday afternoon in September when I was driving home for the last time from my place of work. We had been given plenty of notice that redundancy was coming, but somehow it was always sometime in the future.

Not that day. That was it, no more drive into work. No more regular routine, oh and no more money.

I guess I was mulling over the reality of it all as I approached the 60 mph sign on the motorway. I was accelerating out of the 50 limit and there it was. A police camera van. I'd travelled that road many times but had never seen a speed trap. Why has this bit of motorway got a 50 limit anyhow? I wonder how many drivers have asked that? Perhaps I was caught, perhaps not. I wasn't sure what speed I was doing. I was just following the rest. Now I was in for a two or three week wait. Damn. As if worrying about not having a job wasn't enough.

As I got home, I felt so empty and lonely. It's all so negative. No job. On the dole. Made redundant. I didn't sleep so well that night worrying about it all. I was perhaps luckier than many. I had a little savings and not many debts, but in those early days, negative thoughts outweighed any positive ones.

I was in my mid 50's and irrespective of any anti age discrimination laws, I felt that my age was against me. I almost felt a little embarrassed, in that all my friends had good jobs and I was 'on the scrap heap'. A friend tried to reassure me that redundancy does not mean that you personally were made redundant, it's the job that was made redundant. OK, but same result!

Next morning was Saturday. I remember when I used to look forward to weekends. Now every day will be like a Saturday. It was a lovely sunny day. I thought I would cheer myself up by going for a ride on my bike. I'll dig the Harley out of the garage and go for a run down the motorway to clear my frustration. Just then a horrible thought came over me. If I'm out of work for long, I may have to sell the bike to make ends meet. I felt worse than ever.

So what happens during the first weeks of unemployment? Well it's not that bad actually. Yes there are all the usual worries, but you get to lie in on Monday morning. No joining the traffic jam, or standing on a cold station platform or crowding on to a late bus. You are free. You can stay in bed, watch television, have a late breakfast or do what ever you like. It's almost fun. No boring routine, no nasty boss, no watching the clock and oh yes, no money. I'm afraid the novelty of freedom does not last too long. Reality has a nasty habit of coming up behind you and biting you on the backside.

One of my friends who spent some time out of work said to me 'daytime television is the greatest incentive to get a job!'

So, where is all this going? Well let you tell me a little about myself so as you know who is trying to help you. My background has for many years been in Sales and Marketing. I started off as a Sales Rep. and finished as a Sales Manager. I've always been a bit of an extrovert and quickly found that I could make my living by talking to people.

One day, after sales had not been so good for a while, I thought, 'I don't need all this hassle and I'm fed up driving 150+ miles each day. I'm going for a change of career.' I joined a training organisation, assisting people with the skills of seeking and securing work. I derived great satisfaction out of helping the people whom I taught and eventually I went on to gain a full teaching qualification.

Sadly, the company lost its contract to carry out this training and the staff were made redundant. In between looking for a new job, I have taken time to write this little book in the hope that my experience may help you and others.

Some of the content will appear basic and obvious, but I hope this book will be read by all those who need assistance in getting that first job, returning to work or changing their existing role.

I could list dozens of different jobs and careers. Each person will have an idea of the most suitable type of work for them. Some positions will be the perfect career and others will be chosen simply to live and pay the bills.

If you have ever had a steady job, you will appreciate that we spend a lot of our lives at work. Wouldn't it be really good if we could get a job that we actually liked!

The same basic principles apply no matter what your work aspirations are. *You have to work at looking for work.* Your job is to find a job. Sadly, it's a job without any wages. The old saying 'you don't get anything for nothing' is true. The more effort you put into job hunting, the better chance you have of success.

I propose to assist you in your quest with advice and guidance on such things as: Looking for vacancies, presenting yourself well on the phone, filling in application forms, producing a knockout CV and doing well at the interview. On top of that, I will include snippets of useful information which is geared to pointing you in the right direction.

Be receptive to what is written here. Approach this book in a positive way and read it with an open mind. If you adopt a 'can do' attitude and try your best to read the book from cover to cover, then you will be well on your way to securing the job you want. There is no guarantee with this book, but please remember, it was not written by some theory based academic. It was written by an ordinary guy with the same ups and downs in life as you. The only difference is, I have a professional knowledge of the subject and a passion to get the information over to you.

Enjoy the book. Take it in. Act upon it. Read relevant bits again and good luck in your job quest.

The First Bit

I suppose I'd better tell you the reason for the unusual title. I've had the misfortune to be out of work on a few occasions. I've never enjoyed being unemployed and have always made ongoing applications by sending out my CV both speculatively and to advertised jobs.

Each day I would hopefully await a reply from someone. I remember the days when the post used to come at 7.30 in the morning, with another delivery at lunch time. Now the post appears to be frequently late. Among all the bills and junk mail, there just may have been an invitation for an interview, or a job offer. Sometimes, 'the postman was late.'

One sad fact of life you have to get used to when applying for jobs, is that many companies and organisations just don't appear to have the good manners to reply to your letters.

There are a few basics that you must establish before you start out on this awesome task of getting yourself a job.

Firstly, you have to take it seriously. By that I mean, you must really *want* to get a job. In working to get back into employment, you should commit time, effort and a little money. If you don't, others will!

You certainly need to devote time. Looking for and securing a good job is a time consuming business. It takes time to look for suitable positions, time to prepare and target your CV and time to fill in application forms. Don't do the bare minimum that the *Job Centre* asks you to do. You are not working for the *Job Centre*; you are working for your own future.

You really do need a strong 'got to' factor. You need desire and commitment. You have got to want a job and not just be going through the motions. There may be a lot of jobs out there, but there are also lots of people going after them.

There are obviously many different types of work and people with differing abilities. Some may be able to walk up to a building site and ask the foreman... 'Any bricklayer's jobs going?' After a 10 minute chat you may be asked to start tomorrow. There are other jobs which may require as many as three interviews and a load of qualifications. It could take up to 6 weeks from applying to joining.

When we say you need some effort, that simply means you need to have the discipline to knuckle down to the task of seeking work.

It does not take long after you finish work for the last time, to slip into a comfy, lazy life style of hanging around the house, watching the telly and putting off the nasty business of job seeking to another time.

Effort and Commitment are the keys to a successful job hunt.

What about money? I'm afraid you have got to speculate to accumulate. That simply means when you have little or nothing coming in, you still have to spend money!

What do we need to spend money on? Well, ink for the printer, paper, envelopes, stamps, telephone calls, petrol or fares to travel to interviews and perhaps some new clothes. If you can't type or use the computer, you may need to pay someone to type your CV and letters.

Take a tip from me. Don't wait for the *Benefits Office* to help you. Don't say you can't afford it, just do it. This is your mission and goal. Don't dream up excuses for inaction. If you want the job, pull out all the stops and make the effort.

You may of course think that this is all 'airy fairy' motivational stuff which doesn't apply to you. I *do* live in the real world. I know people who have put a lot of effort into job hunting and have made dozens of applications with no results. Nothing is guaranteed, but this book should give you a definite head start on those who will not have read it or who are too lazy to make the effort. Job hunting is a bit of a 'numbers game'. Don't send out that super CV for the job that is 'just right for you' and sit back waiting to be called for interview. *Send out more and more applications.* As I said, a bit of a numbers game. The more applications, the better the chance. As we know from the gambling world, there is no such thing as a 'dead cert'.

The following pages cover the different aspects of how to look for vacancies and prepare yourself for the application process.

Applying For Jobs -
Making A Start

You can't just decide 'Oh, I'll look for a job today'.
You have got to have some sort of plan to get you from
where you are now, to where you want to be.
Are your goals realistic?
Do you know where to start?

To help you plan your job search, ask yourself the
following questions:

- Are you clear about what sort of work you are
  looking for?
- Do you know what skills, abilities, and
  qualifications you need?
- Are you aware of your own skills and
  abilities?
- Do you have a good Curriculum Vitae (CV) /
  Resume.

- Do you know the places to look for possible vacancies?
- Have you registered with any Recruitment Consultancies / Agencies?
- Do you read the newspaper job sections?
- Does your type of work have a trade or professional journal?
- Have you tried the 'speculative' approach: letters, phone calls?
- Are you confident using the phone to contact potential employers?
- Have you any problem with writing letters?
- Do you know how to fill in an application form well and correctly?
- Do you keep records of the potential employers you have approached?

You see, job searching is not that straight forward. When you seriously consider the above questions, you will see what elements of job search skills you need to concentrate on.

The following pages offer the advice and guidance needed to give you a head start in finding that good job. All the above points are covered in an easy to read format.

Go to it and good luck.

Some Ways to Job Hunt
and Search for Work

I was once told that 'looking for a job is a full time job in its self'

You must devote time to search for work and time to produce a good CV and time to fill out an application form.

If you are serious about job hunting, then you must devote your time over and over again. Apply for lots of suitable positions and keep applying. It may be a pain in the neck, but the reward of *getting that job* is great.

Here are a few ways you may use to look for work:-

THE NEWSPAPER: Check the local and national papers. Check the free papers. Buy the recruitment papers (Yes, you have to spend a little money if you are serious about job search.)

THE INTERNET: If you have a computer, use it. Search jobs within your skill base, or locality. Check company web sites for vacancies. Check specific job search websites. (No computer? Try the library for free Internet use.)

YELLOW PAGES: This publication lists all the specific industries and companies in your area. Use it to get addresses, phone numbers, web sites.

SPECULATIVE LETTERS: Compose a good open letter geared to selling yourself to a potential employer. A speculative letter is a letter sent to a potential employer who has not actually advertised a vacancy.
Send out quite a lot, but be selective. Target specific companies. Give them a ring first and try to get the name of the HR or Department Manager.

COLD CALLING: A bit nerve racking but simply knock on the doors of companies you may be interested in. Go armed with a copy of your CV and be polite. If the boss isn't in, perhaps make an appointment. Get a number.

NETWORKING: This simply means asking colleagues and friends about jobs they may know about within their workplace or elsewhere.

AGENCIES: Job agencies can cover several different fields, or a specific trade or industry. e.g. a 'driver agency'. Their services are free to you. They make money from the employer. Agencies need *you* to make their living, so don't be intimidated by them. Sell your skills. Be keen, but not desperate.

REMEMBER, A high percentage of jobs are there, but are *not* advertised! It's up to you to find these hidden vacancies.

What Are Employers Looking For?

The Employer, Manager, Boss, Interviewer, call them what you like, must not be looked upon as the 'bad guy' or 'enemy'.

They have a task to complete and that is to get the right person for the job.

They are employed by their organisation to choose the best person from all the applicants.

This is done by advertising, checking CV's or application forms and conducting interviews.

The employer is not out to trap you or make you fail the interview.

It's not personal, but he or she must choose wisely, not only for their own sake, but for the benefit of the company.

Apart from specific job requirements, there are some basic things employers are looking for. Here are a few:

To be able to work as part of a team	To learn the job quickly
Demonstrate high personal standards	To be a good time keeper
Able to use your own initiative	To 'go that extra mile'
Trustworthy / Honest	Reliable / Versatile
Able to work on your own	Basic computer skills
Pleasant personality	Able to fit in
Learn from your mistakes	'Think outside the box'
Contribute with new ideas	Not be disruptive
Sense of humour, good	Company clown, not good!

Transferable Skills

What are your Transferable Skills?

These are simply skills, abilities and knowledge which you have gained in previous employment, that you can bring with you to a new job. These skills could also come from college work, life experience or out of work activities. (hobbies/interests)

It's mostly your previous work experience that a potential employer will be interested in.

Use your 'Transferable Skills' to sell yourself to an interviewer.

Please check out the examples listed on the next page. Do you have any of these skills?

IT/Computer skills	Leadership / Management
Good Communication skills	Planning and Organisation
Good with figures	Persuasiveness
Motivating others	Problem solving
Customer relations	People skills
Able to follow instructions	Health & Safety awareness
Able to work as part of a Team	Able to work on my own
Technical knowledge	Written communication
Goal orientated	Ability to adapt

The Speculative Letter

Sent to a prospective employer who has not actually advertised a job.

22 Oak Tree Grove
Oldtown
Ridgegrove
Hampshire
XY5 3BB

The Transport Manager
Speedy Wheels Delivery
Castle Street
Uptown
Hampshire VM10 9QR

7th April 2008

Dear Sir or Madam,

I am writing to enquire as to whether you have any vacancies for a Delivery Driver. Please find enclosed my CV for your consideration.

Briefly, I would like to highlight the following points which I feel may be of interest to you.

- I hold a full, clean driving licence
- Experienced Multi Drop driver
- Fit and in good health
- I am reliable and trustworthy
- Good geographical knowledge of the area
- Available at short notice

I would welcome the opportunity of an interview and look forward to hearing from you shortly.

With thanks.

Yours faithfully,

David Houston

Remember....If you *know* the name of the person, you finish with......*Yours sincerely,*

If you *don't know* the name, i.e. Dear Sir or Madam, finish off with .....*Yours faithfully,*

Guidelines for Writing
a Covering Letter

Whether you are sending a CV on 'spec.' to an employer who has not advertised a job, or enclosing a CV or Application Form in response to an advertised job, it's always good to send a 'Covering Letter'.

What is a Covering Letter?

A covering Letter is simply a short personal introduction, making specific reference to the vacancy / job.

How is the letter made up?

Your address should be at the top right hand corner. This may include your phone number and E-mail, but *not* your name. Please see example on page 25.

The name and address of whom you are sending it to should be on the Left side, but lower than your address.

Don't forget to date it. The date should be on the left, below the employers address.

Use the recipient's title if known.... i.e. The HR Manager.

Paragraph 1 should be the Introduction.

Paragraph 2 should highlight skills and experience for the job.

The last paragraph should 'close' your letter in a polite but firm way. (See example.)

Finish with: *Yours sincerely,* if you know the persons name, or *Yours faithfully,* if you don't.

Don't forget to **sign the letter !**

An imaginary job ad. from the local newspaper.

JOB SECTION

OFFICE ADMINISTRATOR

This is an opportunity to join a dynamic modern office.

A starting salary of £18,000 pa depending on experience.
Additional benefits include – A Non Contributory Pension Scheme. BUPA and 25 days holiday plus Bank Holidays.

Office and computer experience essential, but above all we require a self motivated, positive person with good organisational skills.

Apply in writing, enclosing CV to:

Mr William Rodgers, Sales Director.
Modern Homes Ltd.
73 Old Forge Road,
Market Town,
Hampshire. MM23 7HT

(Closing date for applications: 20th June 2008)

A Covering Letter to go with your CV in reply to the Job ad. in the newspaper.

Tel: 02392 123456   89 Hamilton Avenue
Mob. 07989 345678   Solent
E-mail dprestonxxx@xxx.com   Hampshire
                                                       VR5 7XY

Mr W Rodgers, Sales Director.
Modern Homes Ltd.
73 Old Forge Road
Market Town
Hampshire MM23 7HT

9th June 2008

Dear Mr Rodgers,

Re. Vacancy for Office Administrator

Further to your recent newspaper advertisement regarding the above vacancy, I wish to be considered for the position.

As you can see from the enclosed CV, I have had a successful career in administration, obviously involving considerable office experience. I am Computer Literate and am familiar with a wide range of IT applications.

Being a well organised, self motivated and very positive person, I would relish the opportunity and challenge of working for a company such as yours.

To this end, I look forward to discussing the vacancy with you at interview. I hope to hear from you shortly.
Thanking you.

Yours sincerely,

Derek Preston

                                                    Encl. CV

Your Speculative or Covering Letter

Keep it SHORT !!

Highlight your interest in the job.

Keep it Positive. No negatives!

Check your spelling and grammar.

Sound keen, but not desperate.

Try to avoid the continual use of the word 'I'

Be Clear, Professional and Polite.

End the letter with a 'Thank you' and perhaps....

'I look forward to hearing from you'.

Take time to create the letter. Think how it will look to the employer.

Make sure you sign and date it.

Keep a copy.

Read it over and include it with your CV.

How to Use The Phone to Help You Get an Interview.

So, we all have mobile phones. We use them every day. Why do we need to read an article on how to use a phone?

Don't worry, I'm not going to tell you how to use a phone. What I am going to do is give you a little advice on how to best present yourself on the phone when speaking to a potential employer. Totally different from chatting to your friends.

Remember, speaking on the phone to a potential employer is similar to sending in a CV or Application Form. It is unlikely that you will get a job offer over the phone. The main purpose of the phone call is to try to confirm an interview.

Again, please remember.... *'You don't get a second chance to make a first impression'*

What you have got to do on the phone is: **Convey a Positive Image.**

Believe or not, when talking on the phone, a large part of communication involves the tone of our voice as opposed to what we actually say!
Think of how you will sound to a potential employer listening to your call.
Leave them with a desire to want to meet you.

Tell the employer what you can do, not what you can't.

Here are four words starting with the letter 'P' that are worth thinking about before starting the call:
Try to present yourself as being :-

- POLITE
- PLEASANT
- PROFESSIONAL
- POSITIVE

This may sound corny, but try to *smile* when speaking. Believe me, this will come across.

Using the Phone as a Tool to Find Work

The potential employer may have many calls on a daily basis. You have got to make yours stand out from the rest.

Remember, you will probably only have one chance to make a good first impression!

Here are a few tips to help you.

Prepare yourself before picking up the phone. Have the job advert. and description of the job beside you. Have a copy of your CV. Make sure you have a pen and paper to hand. You may need to write names and numbers. Read the ad. again and understand what the employer is looking for.

Know what you want out of the phone call: Try to get an interview, or if that is not possible, ask if you can send in your CV.

You should read the job description again. Identify what it's about and why you are attracted to it. If you have the required skills, tell them at the start of the conversation. It might be a good idea to rehearse what you are going to say. Avoid waffle!

Find out who you want to speak to. Try to get through to the Manager or Supervisor or who ever will be your senior. Try to get his or her name. If they are not available, say you shall 'call back'. *Don't* leave your name and number for them to call you. It is unlikely that they will. Why should they?

When on the phone, try to speak clearly and with some confidence. Be yourself. You don't need a posh accent. Say what you have to say and 'close' for an interview. The person you are speaking to will think well of you for having the confidence to ask for the Interview. Be enthusiastic, but not desperate!

Think for a few seconds before clearly answering questions. Don't ramble on and on. Remember one of the four 'P's'..... Professional.

Be sure to get the full address of the company along with the name and job title of the manager before hanging up. It may also be useful to get the company e-mail or web address.

Finish the conversation in a professional, friendly and positive way. You may like to say.... 'Thank you for your time, I'll have the CV in the post tonight', or, 'I'll e-mail my CV. What is your e-mail address please.'

Or…. 'Thank you for your time. I'll look forward to seeing you at 11.00 o'clock on Friday.'

If you are making a 'cold call' or 'speculative' call in hope of a potential job, start with your name and give the reason for your call.
Don't go into detail with the receptionist.
Try for the relevant department or ask for 'HR' (Human Resources) or 'Personnel'

If the person you want to speak to is not there, don't leave a message. Find out what time they may be in and say you shall call back.

If there are no vacancies, ask if there may be any vacancies in other departments.
Ask if you can send in your CV.
They may want to send you an Application Form.
Don't forget to get a name, title and address.

End on a positive and friendly note. Always 'leave the door open'. You may be in contact again!

Don't forget to follow up on whatever you have agreed.

Speculative telephone calls are a bit hit and miss. You may be lucky, but be prepared for several rejections. This can be soul destroying and frustrating, especially after many calls. Take a break. Have a tea or coffee.
As with the whole business of job hunting, it's a time consuming numbers game. Keep at it and hopefully your efforts will be rewarded.

Your CV

CV stands for **Curriculum Vitae.** These are two Latin words, roughly translated as..... 'The path or course of life'. In some countries, this document is called a 'Resume'.

More importantly, the CV is a document geared to selling you to an employer. Yes, it's a sales brochure. It may appear crude, but you have to look upon yourself as a commodity which has to be 'sold' to a potential employer.

You may think that the main purpose of a CV is to get you a job. Well, it partially is, but it's main purpose is to get you an Interview.
The Interview comes before the Job and your CV is the only thing which an employer has to judge you on. Make it a good one. Remember..... 'You don't get a second chance to make a first impression'

If you look upon preparing your CV as a complete pain, then it's probably not worth doing. It's got to be as well thought out as the sales brochure for a new car.

On that basis, it should be ....eye catching, dynamic, and easy to read. Only bring out positive things. Don't say – 'I can operate a computer, but I'm not very good at it'. Did you ever see a car advert. which said.... 'Oh by the way, this car is prone to rust and sometimes the engine cuts out'.
You wouldn't buy the car, would you?! It's the same with the CV. Keep it positive!

Your CV has got to stand out from the rest

What then does the recruiter / employer do with the CV?

Hopefully, they read it. It could be a quick glance to see if it's worth reading in full. If it does not stand out, or the qualifications don't match, or if it's too long, then it is likely to be put on the 'NO' heap. You will *not* be called for interview.

If it looks good, is well laid out and easy to read then you stand a good chance of being asked to attend for an interview.
The potential employer simply wants to know if the applicant has the skills, experience, qualifications and enthusiasm for the job. 'Is the job right for the person?' 'Is the person right for the job?' 'Will they fit in?'
The employer is not there to fail you; they just want the best person for the job.

The interviewer will only know as much about you as you choose to tell on the CV. This is the only basis which he or she has to go on, in deciding who shall be called for interview. (The interviewer may also have an Application Form which you filled in, but that's for another section)

Here is a good tip. You need to produce a *Functional CV*.....This is a 'general' one which you could give to any potential employer. Sometimes though, it's better to take your Functional CV and tweak it to make a *Targeted CV*. It's the same document, but altered to suit the actual job you are applying for.

Remember, the interviewer will work out some of the questions he/she may ask you at interview from your CV details. Make sure you don't tell any blatant lies that you can't back up!

As you can see, the CV is a very important document. It should be neat, in logical order and presented in a professional way. Word process it. Check the grammar and spelling. If you are not sure, get a friend to read it over.
Don't make it difficult for the employer to read or extract information from. Follow these steps:

Make sure it attracts attention and encourages the employer to want to meet you.

Have it typed on good quality paper. White or light coloured, not lime green! (That's not what we mean when we say 'make it stand out')

Ideally, it should not exceed 2 pages in length. You will have an opportunity to list all your skills and qualifications on the application form.

Don't try to impress with Jargon. Use plain English.

Encourage speed reading. Avoid using long 'flowery' sentences.

I would suggest you write it in the 1st person. (As though you are writing it yourself and not as though someone else has written it.)

Include 'bullet points' and bold script.

A few tips:

Make sure your name stands out, but don't print it in huge type.

Give your full postal address along with land line, mobile number and e-mail if you have one. (I would advise not to include your e-mail address if it's too weird or rude!)

Use your date of birth, not your age. (age is ok if you are under 30, but don't rely on the Age Discrimination Act!)

You don't really need marital status or number of children.

(Saying things like 'Divorced' or 'Single parent' could possibly be perceived as negative.)

If you have to write your nationality, it's British if you were born in the UK.....*Not* 'English' or any other country that makes up the UK!

<u>Your Education</u> – Put the most recent qualifications first. My advice is, if you got an 'E' or 'F' in any GCSE's, leave them out.

If you do not have any GCSE's, don't write 'No qualifications.' That looks bad. Write, 'Good all round Secondary education' or, 'Educated to GCSE standard.'

<u>Career</u>, otherwise known as 'Job History.'

Always work backwards. Start with your last job and list back to whenever you choose. (No real need to go back much over 10 years.)

You may get away with giving the year(s) only for your periods of work. This makes the time in employment look longer than including the day and month.

<u>Interests</u>: Try not to refer to these as 'hobbies' and try to make them relevant. Relate them to your *transferable skills*. i.e. Treasurer, Secretary, Chairperson, Youth Worker etc. If you are into sport, mention just a few, not a long list. You may be able to talk about your social interests for ages, but the interviewer is not really interested. Think how you will come across to the employer. Don't let the interviewer think you spend all day playing computer games, or in the pub, or talking about football. On the other hand, don't try to impress by saying you play golf

when you have never been any further than the local putting green!

Lastly:-

The Personal Profile......Think this out carefully -

Make it Detailed. To the point. Hard hitting but *not too long*.

Many CV's are very similar. <u>It's the Personal Profile that will make yours stand out</u>.

The Personal Profile is the bit where you really have a chance to sell yourself and relate your CV to the job.

Put some thought into it. Do a rough draft. Add to it. Change it. Make it a work of art!

Use Bullet Points to highlight Key Points, Skills, Qualifications etc.

Remember, no one ever gets a job by simply submitting a CV.

The CV is the key to the Interview door. Once you are in the door, the CV has done its work. It gives you a foundation to help secure the job.

Personal Qualities

Do any of these words describe you?
(You may like to use some of these words in your
Personal Profile)

ADAPTABLE	DECISIVE
WILLING	THOROUGH
PRECISE	CARING
ENERGETIC	HONEST
HARD WORKING	DEDICATED
RESPONSIBLE	SUPPORTIVE
TRUSTWORTHY	ORGANISED
FLEXIBLE	FRIENDLY
HUMOROUS	CREATIVE
COMMITTED	PERSUASIVE
HELPFUL	IMAGINATIVE
SENSITIVE	PRODUCTIVE
GOOD TIME KEEPER	RELIABLE

Your Skills and Strengths

Do any of these words describe you?
Can you use any of these words to add to your
CV, Application Form or Personal Profile?

I am a good 'Team Player'	Able to work in a group
I can work unsupervised	I can use my own Initiative
Hard Working	Reliable
A good Time Keeper	Punctual
IT / Computer literate	Understanding Systems
Trustworthy	Honest
Supervisory skills	Management experience
I am Self Confident	Competent and Efficient
I can work under Pressure	I can follow Instructions
Responsible / Consistent	Attention to Detail
Customer Service experience	Helping / Advising others

Good at working with my Hands	Motivated
Good Communication skills	Organisational ability
Experience in Leading a group	Motivating people
Training people	A good sense of Humour

Your CV Check List

What is the Purpose of your CV?	To convince the employer that:
	You can do the Job.
	You have the necessary experience.
	The Job will suit you.
	You will 'fit in'
The CV should…..	*Attract Attention!*
	Encourage the interviewer to want to meet you.

Presentation:	It should be typed on good quality white or light coloured paper.
	Ideally, not exceed 2 pages in length.
	Do not use 'Jargon'
	Encourage - speed reading.
	Be written in the 1st person... By yourself.
	Include 'Bullet Points' and bold type.
	Be easy to read, in correct order and neat & tidy.
Your Personal Profile:	This should highlight important facts and achievements along with key strengths and skills.
Two types of CV:	Functional.....General CV
	Targeted...Aimed at a specific job.

Your CV Check List. A few notes:

We mentioned the word **'Jargon'**. What is Jargon?

The Dictionary describes 'Jargon' as –

'Specialised language concerned with a particular subject.'

For example, think of all the words associated with computers..... Mouse, Motherboard, Hard-drive, Megabite, etc. and hundreds more. If you knew nothing about computers, this 'jargon' would mean nothing to you.

Think of the Navy….. Port, Starboard, Bow, Stern, Fore & Aft. etc. and hundreds more nautical words. If you were not familiar with the sea and ships, this lot would mean nothing.

Jargon relates to specific terms within certain jobs or industry. You will not impress anyone if you use this terminology out of context. Just avoid it.

We also mentioned **'Bullet Points'**

Bullet points are simply dots at the start of a series of 'key points', set out to emphasise a list of important features which you wish to draw attention to.

The bullet points are indented from the normal script and can be created by pressing the relevant 'bullet point' icon on the computer's tool bar.

Don't do too many. 6 to 8 are best to get a good impact.

Try to keep the key point to one line and make it 'punchy'

The notes say: Encourage **'Speed Reading'**

What does Speed Reading mean?

Let's face it, a lot of us are lazy readers. That's why we all watch more TV than engage in reading.

The potential employer will have lots of CV's to read. They don't have the time or inclination to read your life history. They need to see the main points that relate to you and your ability to do the job.

If you are in your 40's there is need to go into detail about your primary school!

The people who best encourage *speed reading* are newspaper editors. Every newspaper has to compete with others on the news stand to be bought by the reader. I would suggest that if the front page were all in column inches and a tiny typeface, no one would bother buying it.

Look at the front pages….. Big bold writing, a photograph, a different type face, perhaps some colour. See what I'm getting at…. Something that grabs you.

I'm *not* suggesting you present your CV like a newspaper front page, but make it stand out. Punchy and to the point.

Using 'speed reading' simply makes it easier to read, and we all like things to be easier, even employers!

What do we mean by being **'Written in the 1st Person?'**

This is an English grammar terminology which means the CV is / appears to be written by yourself. This differs from *'The 3rd Person'* which is where it appears that someone else is writing it for you.

Let me give you an example :-

'I consider myself to be an honest and hardworking person'

That's 1st person, using the word 'I'. In other words, writing about myself.

If your CV said - 'David is an honest and hardworking person', that is as though someone else has written it for you. That's 3rd person.

It's your choice, but I prefer the 1st Person.

Completing Application Forms

Let's get one thing straight from the start. Filling in application forms is an absolute pain in the neck. It's long, time consuming and a real task if you have to complete it 'longhand' i.e. filling it in by pen as opposed to typing it on a computer.

Sadly, application forms are part of the job search process, so we either accept them or stop looking for a job. In many occasions, we have a nicely prepared CV, so we have to ask, 'why do I have to repeat all the information again on an application form?' Let me explain the difference.

A CV is what *you* want to tell the employer. An Application Form is what *the employer* wants to know from you. See the subtle difference?

On the CV you may have a little poetic licence, but on the application form, you have to answer all the questions accurately.

There are a couple of basics you must appreciate regarding the application form. Firstly, it will take time to fill in. That is probably at least an hour or more. Appreciate this and allow time to complete it properly. It must also be completed in a neat and tidy way. That means taking your time to write or type neatly. It's not a five minute job! The application form is every bit as much a selling tool as your CV. Don't look upon it as a pain. Look upon it as an excellent opportunity to promote yourself. *The application form is an important tool to help you secure the interview.*

Here are a few hints to help you complete the application form:

(1) **Take a Photocopy of the blank Application Form.** Mistakes or corrections do not make a good impression. Use the photocopy to do a 'rough draft' and then use it to help complete the original.

(2) **Match yourself to the job.** Check the 'job specification' and 'person profile'. Pay attention to the main requirements, skills and responsibilities etc. The more 'boxes you can tick' the better chance of being shortlisted.

(3) **Read the blank application form before writing anything.** Be aware of such instructions as: 'Please complete in Block Capitals' or perhaps, 'Please complete in Black Ink'

As you read each section, assess what the employer is trying to find out.

(4) **Stand out from the crowd**. If you have any special skills or abilities that are relevant to the job, make sure you mention them. Emphasise your best qualifications, making sure you mention the most relevant ones first. If you have a Degree or NVQ, don't start with your GCSE's or 'O' levels.

(5) **Stress your positive qualities**. Stress your strong points and achievements. Tell the employer what they want to know. Ensure it promotes you in the best possible light. Try not to include negatives;

Don't say 'I can work a computer, but I'm not very good'. Remember, a positive attitude does show and it may make a difference.

(6) **Don't leave 'fields' or spaces, empty.** Make sure you always put something in the space provided, even if it does not apply. If you leave it blank because you think the question is not relevant to you, the employer may think you have missed it, or just couldn't be bothered filling it in. You may know it doesn't apply, but the employer doesn't know that.

If the question does not apply to you, write N/A (not applicable)

(7) **Be Honest!** Remember, you have to sign the form at the bottom saying that it is filled in accurately, to the best of your knowledge. A blatant lie could result in dismissal or perhaps even prosecution. Don't make claims you can't substantiate. You will get questions at the interview based

on your application form, and it takes a liar to have a good memory!

(8) **Don't leave huge time gaps in your work history**. If you were unemployed, say so. There is no shame in that these days. Remember, a time gap could be explained by taking time off work to go abroad, or looking after a sick or elderly relative. I once left a long time between job dates on my CV and was asked at interview if I was 'in jail'!

If you can get away with it, state employment times in years only, not months and years.

(9) **Create a good first impression**. Remember we said earlier, *'you only get one chance to make a good impression'* Take time to produce a neat, tidy and well completed application form.

Don't rush it. If it's worth doing, it's worth doing well. Remember it's your selling tool to get an interview and hopefully that good job.

(10) **Approach the people whom you are going to give as a Reference.** All job applications will require references. Don't just write down someone who you assume will give you a reference. Have the good manners to contact them and ask if they would be kind enough to give you a reference for a job application. Get their Name, Address, Phone number and if possible E-mail.

The best person to get a reference from is your previous manager or boss. If you can't do that, then ask your old teacher or college lecturer. Perhaps a clergyman or policeman or probation officer or doctor or any 'responsible' member of society. Your mum, dad, brother or sister do not count!

(11) **Don't forget to sign and date it.** Just don't forget this!

(12) **When the form is complete, read it over again**. Check for mistakes. This is important. No one is perfect.

(13) **When you have finished, take a photocopy of the completed form.** Keep a photocopy or save it on the computer. It will be useful to take to the interview.

Here's an important tip: If you are applying for jobs on a regular basis, you will have many application forms to fill in. Since the questions are so similar, keep an original copy so as you can simply transfer the information to the new form.

(14) **Get it in the post, or E-mail it….Now!** Be aware of 'closing dates for application' Get it on to the boss's desk as soon as possible.

One final piece of advice. Don't try to take the easy way out with the questions. Analyse what the employer is trying to ascertain in asking the question. Give them what they want. Know the job you are going for and sell your skills. Make your answers clear and to the point. Don't waffle. Remember the employer has lots of application forms to read. Don't bore them with your life history or too much information. You can expand on the answers at the interview.

In conclusion, while it may be a pain filling in application form after application form, remember, this is your selling tool to secure that vital interview. Either do it with a willing heart, or don't do it at all. If you want the job, it's got to be done and done well. Remember, there will be others who couldn't be bothered, so you'll be ahead of them!

The Job Interview

THE THREE MOST IMPORTANT THINGS
ABOUT A SUCCESSFUL INTERVIEW
PREPARATION PREPARATION PREPARATION

Basic Preparation

Where is the interview to take place?
How do I get there?......Public transport, Map, Car parks.
Where in the building is the interview?
What is the name of your interviewer?
What do I need to take with me? … Copy of CV,
References, Certificates. *

Specific Preparation

Read your CV and Application form again.
Think of any questions they may ask.
Have specific questions to ask them.
What do you know about the company?
Where do you find this information? - Internet, Company
brochures, Job ad.
What do you know about the job?

Tips for the interview

<u>Don't be Late</u>.   If you can't make it or are going to be late through no fault of your own, phone the company and explain.

Create a good first impression.

Be neat & tidy : Suit or Smart casual depending on the job.

Be polite and friendly.

If you have to wait, read any literature available.

* You may also be asked to bring : Proof of right to work in the UK.

Your Driving Licence, Passport or National Insurance number.

Remember, an interviewer is not out to trap you or make you feel bad. They simply want the right person for the job. They are not any better or worse than you. The interviewer should be professional, fair and respectful. You should be the same.

At The Interview

A few Do's -

Smile, respond to the interviewer's greeting and shake hands.
Sit when asked and remember your body language. (see 'body language' in the next section)
Try to relax and be yourself.
Remember, this is the chance to sell yourself.
Stress your achievements, skills and knowledge.
Avoid negative points about yourself.
Be interested in what the interviewer has to say and listen carefully.
Give full answers.

* Close properly. (please see page 60)

A few Don'ts -

Don't be late!
Don't drink alcohol beforehand.
Don't smoke while waiting or during the interview.
Don't give short answers.
Don't be critical of past employers.
Don't argue.
Don't try to be funny or make jokes.
Don't use bad language.
Don't interrupt the interviewer.
Switch your mobile phone off!

It's good to take a mint, or chew gum before the interview to freshen up, but *don't* eat or chew during the actual interview.

* A suggested way of closing the interview when the interviewer has indicated 'that's it'

'Thank you for giving me the opportunity of talking with you.
I have been very impressed with both the company and the position.
I hope I have convinced you that I am the right person for the job.
I look forward to hearing from you shortly.'
With that, shake hands and say 'Thanks again, goodbye'
Don't say anything after that, just leave.

Let's look at a few of these do's and don'ts

At the start, the greeting is important. Respond to the interviewer's greeting in a friendly way. Look at the interviewer, not at the floor. A smile would be good.

One bit of advice on shaking hands. Just give a normal 'positive' handshake. Don't try to impress with a 'bone crusher'. This definitely won't impress. On the other hand, don't present a 'wet lettuce'!

When we say 'relax and be yourself' this may sound easier said than done. Remember, it's a job interview. It shouldn't be a life and death situation. If you don't get the job, it's not the end of the world. The more you relax, the more confident and positive you shall appear. You will be able to recall your experiences and be better able to answer questions. You must of course present yourself in the best light, so you need to be conscious of how you appear to the interviewer, but don't dramatically alter your personality.

Pay attention to what the interviewer is asking. Answer the question asked. Don't waffle. The interviewer may 'lead you' with a line of questioning. Try to understand what the interviewer is getting at. Listen carefully.

When questioned, give full answers. The interviewer does not want to have to drag the answers out of you. The interviewer wants a reasonably in depth answer. The way you answer gives you an excellent opportunity to 'sell' yourself. Don't give 'Yes' – 'No' answers.

It's so obvious to say 'don't be late' for your interview. Arriving on time shows good manners, punctuality and keenness. Having said that, don't go the other way and arrive half an hour too early. That's just silly.

Smoking and drinking. Both are evident by their smell and it certainly does not show you in a positive light. Again, 'first impressions last'. It's wrong to give the impression of drinking during the day, even if it's 'just one'. The employer will not know how many you may have had.

Smoking is virtually banned these days and there are so many people who are very anti smoking. Don't give them an excuse. Don't smoke before the interview.

Don't ever criticise your previous employers....even if they were horrible. It sounds like 'sour grapes' and makes you look unprofessional.

Don't ever argue with the interviewer, even if you know you are right. You'll 'win the battle but lose the war'. In other words, you won't get the job. Keep focused. You are out to secure the job. Don't say or do anything that could jeopardise that goal.

Having a good sense of humour is a positive thing in the workplace, but don't act the clown at the interview, even if it is informal and more light-hearted. Keep up a professional appearance. That does not mean you should be very serious and miserable. Respond to the interviewer in an appropriate way, but no rude or silly jokes.

Don't ever use bad language at the interview. Even if you are on a building site, or in the docks and bad language is part of the culture, don't be tempted to let the odd word slip. If you get the job, and colourful language is an everyday occurrence, then you can swear like a trooper, but not at the interview.

Most of us like to talk and most of us have opinions that we like to get across. Most of us also think that what we have to say is more important than what anyone else has to say. For goodness sake, don't be tempted to interrupt the interviewer. He or she will take a dim view of you talking over them. The interviewer likes to think they are in control of the interview. Don't disillusion them.

This last point is an important one. Most of us carry a mobile phone. For many the 'mobile' is part of their everyday life. Believe it or not, there was a time not so long ago when we lived without mobile phones. Nothing is so important that you need your phone during an interview. *Turn it off.* Don't forget. Just turn it off. It really is considered the height of bad manners for the mobile to go off during the interview. (NB. In many countries outside the UK, the 'mobile' is referred to as a 'Cell phone'.)

One final tip - Say all you have to say during the interview. As mentioned on the previous page, once you say 'goodbye', shut-up, say no more and leave the interview room. Don't be tempted to restart the conversation. That's fatal!

Remember….. Engage the brain before the mouth!

Questions You May be Asked at The Interview

1 Tell me about your self.
2 Give me a brief resume of your work history.
3 What do you know about our company ?
4 What do you think the job involves ?
5 What do you feel you could bring to our company ?
6 What motivates you ?
7 Tell me about a success or major achievement in your working life.
8 How long do you anticipate working here ?
9 Are you a good 'team player' ?
10 Why do you want to work for this company ?
11 What is your idea of success ?
12 Why are you leaving your present job ?
13 What have you learnt from your mistakes ?
14 How do you handle criticism ?
15 What are your strengths ?
16 What are your weaknesses ?

17 What Salary / Wages are you looking for ?

18 Would you have a problem working for a Female / Male boss ?

19 Your manager may be younger than you. Would that be a problem ?

20 If we appointed you, when would you be able to start ?

How Do We Answer These Questions?

1 Tell me about yourself – Try to answer in a business like way. Make the answer relate to your ability to do the job. Don't go on and on about your passion for football.

2 Your Work History – Positive points only. Success stories. No negatives.

3 Knowledge of the company you are applying to – Learn something. Do your research. Check the web site or company brochure.

4 What does the job involve – Know and understand what the job involves. Check the Job Spec. or Person Profile. Speak confidently about the role.

5 What can you bring to us? – Refer to your transferable skills. Extract information from your personal profile. 'Sell' yourself.

6 What motivates you? – No harm in saying 'money', but add a few other things that involve success and helping others.

7 Success in your working life – Think about times you beat your targets or helped someone. Think of a positive contribution you made to your employer.

8 How long do you anticipate working here? – Answer: 'for as far into the future as I can see.' Don't say 'until something better comes along'. You won't get the job!

9 Are you a good Team Player? – This simply means, 'can you work with others' and be part of a 'team'. It's got nothing to do with football!

10 Why do you want to work for us? – Again, do your company research. Mention some positive things about the company.

11 Your idea of success – Tell them what they want to hear. Tell about a work related success story.

12 Why are you leaving your present job? – Have a good reason. Don't ever say 'you were sacked'. Don't ever criticise your previous employer.

13 What have you learnt from your mistakes? – Don't say 'I never make any'. The answer to the question is: 'Not to make the same mistake again.'

14 How do you handle criticism? – You accept it, provided it's helpful and constructive. You are always open to learn and improve.

15 Your strengths – This question gives you an excellent opportunity to 'sell' yourself to the

interviewer. Think of all those positive things you wrote on your CV.

16 Your weaknesses – A much more difficult question, but be prepared for it. Try to turn a negative into a positive. We all have weaknesses, but don't admit something that will fail you. For example, *don't* say…. 'I have difficulty getting out of bed in the morning!'

17 Salary / Wages expected – Have an idea before the interview of the going rate. Don't ask for an unrealistically high figure, but on the other hand, don't undersell yourself.

18 Would you have a problem working for a boss of the opposite sex? – The simple answer is: 'No', if you want the job.

19 Could you work for a younger manager? – Answer: 'Yes'

20 When would you be able to start? – The answer they want to hear is…'As soon as possible', or 'next Monday'. You may have to give a weeks or a months notice, but you should indicate that you are available when needed.

Questions to Ask The Interviewer

Towards the end of the interview, the interviewer will most likely say :-

'Are there any questions you would like to ask?'

Don't say 'No' That may indicate you 'know it all' or are not really interested.

Questions you may ask could be :

- What will be my responsibilities?
- Who will I report to?
- Are there any opportunities for advancement?
- Will there be any training involved?
- Will there be a trial or probationary period?
- Where is the company going. Does the future look good?
- Will relocation be required now or in the future?

- Apart from the necessity for the work to be done in an efficient way, is the company an enjoyable and pleasant place to work?
- When do you expect the appointment to be taken up?
- What is the next step. Is there a second interview?

Not all these questions will be relevant. There may be many more questions that are not listed here. Some of them may have been covered in the interview. The point is, show interest by having a few questions.

NB. During the course of the interview, you should be given information regarding the employment conditions. This could include pay, holidays etc. If the interviewer does not mention holidays, I would strongly advise that you *do not* ask about holidays or time off.

Everyone is entitled to holidays these days. If you ask, the employer may think you are more interested in time off, than being at work!

How do We Present Ourselves at The Interview?

Have you ever met someone who has not actually done you any harm, but you simply don't 'warm' to them. You can't put a finger on it, but you see them as 'not your cup of tea' even after only knowing them for a short time.

An interview can be a bit like this. We all have our personal likes and dislikes. An interviewer / employer should, we assume be professional and only be interested in our ability to do the job. Interviewers are of course human too and they have their likes and dislikes.

If you get as far as being invited for interview, then you are in with a good chance. Your CV or application form has impressed the employer enough to make them want to meet you. It's up to you to take full advantage of this opportunity to sell yourself. We have mentioned this in previous pages, but we now have to ask.... *'How will I present myself at interview?'*

Please remember this, if you remember nothing else :-

First Impressions Last.

Go back to the first paragraph. Remember the person who was 'not your cup of tea'. He or she could have been a perfectly nice person but something about 'the first impression' didn't quite endear them to you.

An interviewer will form an opinion of you within the first 60 seconds of meeting. In many cases even before you have spoken.

How then do we make a good first impression?   You have got to look at your style of dress. How you carry yourself. What you first say. Your manners, attitude and body language.

Let's look at the way we could dress for the interview. A smart suit will certainly make a good impression, but choose it carefully. If you are attending a business interview, don't wear something you feel looks good at the night club. Don't dig out the old suit you last wore for your wedding 20 years ago. If the job is important enough to you and if you may be attending several interviews, don't be mean. Go and buy yourself a new suit.

If you are male, then a more 'sober' suit is probably best. Think carefully about the shirt and tie. Don't ever wear an old dirty tie. Chuck it out. Get a new one. Same with the shirt.

Talking about ties, it can be bright and modern, but not too loud. Don't be tempted to wear one of those cartoon ties. They make you look unprofessional and silly. How can any interviewer take you seriously when they are staring at some grinning cartoon character around your neck?

If the job is worth going for, invest a little cash to look good and don't forget the shoes. There's nothing worse than well worn scruffy shoes and avoid brown shoes with a navy or grey suit! While we are in the feet department, don't ever wear white socks. White socks are for playing tennis or some other sports, but not for an interview. That also goes for the silly cartoon or football socks your son bought you for Father's Day!

A good tip is to look in the mirror just before you leave the house and say to yourself…. 'Would I employ this person?'

The ladies must observe the same guidelines. Certain things must be taken into consideration and I'm not being in any way sexist when I say this. I have interviewed many women and a few have tried to use their feminine charms. Perhaps one button lower undone on the blouse, or the skirt hiked up a few inches.

Most professional / sensible interviewers won't fall for this. Instead, they may think that these actions are being used to hide some shortcomings in the ability to do the job. If these tactics did work, you have got to ask yourself, 'do I actually want to work for this man?' Certainly there is no harm in a woman presenting herself in an attractive way, but avoid engaging in any flirtatious actions.

One important note for the men reading this. Give a female interviewer every bit as much respect as a male interviewer. In a male dominated world, women have always had a harder job to climb the company ladder. If a woman achieves a senior position, then she has probably had to work harder than any male to get there. Don't ever adopt a superior, patronising, dismissive or flirty attitude.

We know of course, that a suit is not always the correct clothing for an interview. You'd probably scare the foreman if you went for a job on a building site in your suit and tie.

The rule of thumb is; always look your best. This could mean 'smart casual', or even jeans and open neck shirt for certain jobs, but make sure they are clean jeans and shirt!

'Body language' was mentioned in the last section. My advice is not to get too hung up on this, but be aware of how your actions and movements come across. Although a lot has been written about body language, it's not an exact science. There are of course a few common sense points -

Don't slouch. Don't adopt an aggressive pose, perhaps with arms folded. Don't stare at the ceiling or look around. Avoid irritating little habits…. You know what I mean. Don't ever look at your watch. Do look interested, professional and positive. Come across as relaxed and confident.

One last little point. It's not for me to dictate how anyone should dress or present themselves, but there are a few basic common sense rules that should be observed. One of these unwritten rules relates to Tattoos and Piercings.

Now I know these have become a lot more common and acceptable in recent days, in both men and women, but when attending an interview, it might be wise not to flaunt them too much.

Obviously there are certain jobs where tattoos and piercings present no problem, but for other positions, especially 'customer facing' roles, these are considered unacceptable. Females can perhaps get away with more piercings than men, but in many cases, 'Health and Safety' issues come into play.

The best advice relating to tattoos is to wear a long sleeve shirt and cover them up. As for nose studs or rings or any other piercings, my advice is to take them out. I am not saying you are wrong to have a tattoo or piercing, but please think how it may look to a potential employer or interviewer.

I'll repeat, *First Impressions last.*

In the previous pages there are notes regarding the actual interview, but always remember that the employer is not only looking for someone who can do the job, but also someone who can fit in.

Remember your manners. Good manners do not mean you have to put on 'airs and graces'. Good manners are common sense.

Remember, **You only get one chance to make a first impression.**

Don't ruin it.

I was once given good advice by an HR manager. She said: 'Remember, God gave us two eyes, two ears and one mouth. Use them in that proportion!'

One last little point about interviews. Do please remember that an interview is a two way exercise. You shouldn't be going along cap in hand saying 'Give us a job mate'. You should be checking them out, just as they are checking you out. Hopefully you are not so desperate that you will take any old job. Do the research and ask questions to make sure you would be happy in the job.

After The Interview

What do we do when the interview is finished? Before you relax, it might be worth while analysing how it went.

When an interview finishes, the interviewer could conclude in several ways. Some people may get offered the job there and then with an offer to start 'tomorrow' or 'Monday', but that does not happen very often.

In most cases the interviewer will say that there are several other people to interview and we shall let you know by 'Friday', or 'within a week.'

Just like when you took an exam at school, you may have a rough idea of how well you did. The unknown factor is, what skills, qualifications or personal attributes the other interviewees may have.

You may or may not get the job, but whatever the result, attending an interview is good practice for the next one.

Many of us come out of an interview saying…I wish I had said this or that, or I wish I had asked that question. Such thoughts may help in preparation for the next interview, but don't dwell on them too long. Again, like a school exam, if you have done the correct preparation, then you can do no more.

With an interview over, there may be a temptation to sit back and wait for good news. Don't! The rule is to keep applying and line up the interviews. Remember, the business of job hunting is a 'numbers game'. The more applications, the better chance you should have.

There is no such thing as a 'dead cert'. Keep looking.

There is another consideration that you need to take into account if you have not been successful in securing a job within your established field. You may have to broaden your outlook and perhaps consider positions from outside your normal skill base. This may appear a little drastic, but if you can't get the actual position you want, go for something else that you feel may suit. This will give you work and money and enable you to be a little more relaxed while looking for something you really want.

Here is a weird fact of life: It is easier to get a job from the strength of already being in employment, as opposed to being unemployed!

The 'rule of thumb' is simple. Keep applying until you actually get a job offer. Once you are secure in a job, then you are free to apply for 'something better' should the opportunity arise.

Large Company Structure

You may ask yourself, 'what has Large Company Structure got to do with me?' If you are looking for work, it may have a lot to do with you.

Some job seekers assume that if they can't do what the company's main production is, then it's not worth approaching them for possible work.

For example:

'I live near a large shipyard on the south coast. I'm not a shipwright, therefore there is no point in approaching this shipyard.'

Or….

'I also live close to a well known manufacturer of Vans. I've no experience on a car/van production line, therefore there's no point in approaching them.'

What we have to do here is what's called 'thinking outside the square'. This simply means, to see the bigger picture. We must realise that there are many departments within a large organisation that although part of the overall production operation, do require different skills.

I would like you to think of as many different departments as you can that form a large company. We can think of obvious ones like the factory floor and perhaps end up with more obscure departments like the Post Room.

Listed below, are a few of the departments that form a medium to large company:

Factory floor / production line	The Maintenance dept.
The IT dept.	Research & Development
HR / Personnel	Salaries & Wages
Management	Accounts dept.
Security	Canteen
Warehouse – goods in/out	Packing / Dispatch
Administration	Transport
Sales & Marketing	PR & Advertising
Buying dept.	Finance
Training	Health & Safety
Post Room	Sports & Social Club
Cleaning	Drawing Office

These are some departments, there may be others. If we look at the factory floor alone, we could fill a page with departments, from the Assembly Line to the Paint Shop etc.

The simple objective of this little exercise is to show that you don't have to be a shipbuilder to work in a shipyard, or a car assembly worker to work in a car plant. The same applies with other medium to large companies.

Look at all the departments within a large organisation and see the many job opportunities that present themselves within such companies. Surely some of your experience or transferable skills could be used in one of these different roles?

If you are not qualified to do the job which is actually advertised within a large company, think of other possibilities and look into that company a little deeper. Are there any other vacancies within the company? Obviously you don't need to be a skilled assembly worker to be a bar person in the company Sports & Social club. Check it out.

If they are taking on people for one department, perhaps they have just secured a big order and need to take on people in other departments to service the order.

Have a go. Contact them. They can only say 'no', but they might say 'yes, please send us your CV'. If you don't try, you will never know.

Obstacles to Getting Work

While it is correct that to succeed in searching for work we should adopt a positive attitude, we must accept that some people have certain barriers to trying.

I feel we must address a few of the issues which could adversely affect the enthusiasm with which some people might seek, or alternatively, not seek work.

These obstacles could be real or imagined. They could be very serious or quite simple and easily overcome.

Let's look at a few:

Age	Race / colour
Having children	Disability
Sickness / Medical condition	Criminal record
Lack of Qualifications	Language difficulties
Long term Unemployment	Travel / distance
Problems with Literacy or Numeracy	No driving licence
Lack of confidence	No Money
Lack of Experience	Alcohol / Drug abuse

These are a few, but I'm sure there are many more. Some are very difficult to overcome, like having a criminal record. With others, you just have to try to find a way around them. This may seem an impossible task, but the job market has many examples of people who have overcome their difficulties and secured a job.

Perhaps the person in a wheelchair shouldn't look for a job as a steeplejack, or the person who has problems with numeracy, shouldn't go for a job as an accountant, but there is work for virtually everyone in some field

In many cases people with real or perceived barriers to work have to dig deep into their own being, to not only find out what suits them, but to be brave enough to apply.
It's a fact of life that in spite of many anti discrimination laws, an employer will probably employ exactly the person they want.
Let's look at a few situations:

The person who thinks they may be too old, can sell themselves on having years of experience and loyalty. The young person has enthusiasm, stamina and an open mind to offer.

If you haven't got the relevant qualifications, there are hundreds of college courses geared to everything from GCSE's to trade skills and more.

Think outside the square a little. If you are low on cash, or haven't got a car, look for something nearer home.

If you have been out of work for over a year, read this book again and plan a new fresh approach. Get help with preparing a new CV. Imagine a bright new 'you' with a job!

If you are new to this country, check out an ESOL course to help you with your English. Ability to speak English well, will double your chances of getting work.

Don't be embarrassed if you are not good at Literacy or Numeracy. Perhaps you've got problems with reading, writing or basic arithmetic. There are college classes where others will be in the same situation. Check them out.

If you have a medical problem, then you should seek a job which will not affect your condition. Obviously, I'm not talking about a serious condition which may prevent you from doing any work at all.

Regarding Disability, there are laws against discrimination in this field. Some companies display a 'Positive about Disability' sign. Having said that, the disabled person should be honest with themselves about what they can and can't do.

Some people may be in the dilemma of having to balance their benefits with a possible wage. 'Is it worth going to work?' The answer has got to be 'yes'.

If you are in doubt, please check with the benefit agencies. You may be able to work and still receive certain benefits. e.g. Working Tax Credits or other payments. It's better to be working, than on benefit, for many reasons.

Lack of experience is a difficult one. You can only console yourself with the obvious fact that we all had to start somewhere. Employers should realise this. Try for an apprenticeship, or start at a lower level.

Lone parents who want to return to work are also in a difficult situation. Child care is expensive. There is government legislation covering this. Check with the benefits people to see if they can help. Many people fit work around children, but I know it's not easy.

For some jobs you need a Driving Licence. The problem is that lessons are expensive. Perhaps you should go for a job that does not require a licence and save up for lessons. I'm afraid the only answer to this one is to get the appropriate licence for the type of vehicle you wish to drive or operate.

For people who feel that having a problem with Alcohol or Drug abuse will prevent them getting a job, then I have to say, it might. People in this situation should perhaps seek help from their doctor or other professionals if they want guidance with this problem.

If you are unfortunate enough to have a criminal record, then there will be many jobs which you simply can't go for. The fact is, you have to declare it. Having said that, it shouldn't be anyone else's business. If you have paid your debt to society and you want to put it behind you, there are agencies out there to help - NACRO, or Citizens Advice. There are of course jobs in which your circumstances can be accepted.

I would have to say that each of these obstacles to work demand more than the few lines written here. Some of these situations require a greater level of guidance and analysis.

For almost all of these circumstances, there are professionals at hand to help you. Having these problems does not make you a second class citizen, even if it feels like it sometimes. You know your circumstances. The situation you are in will not disappear overnight, but I have to assume that you genuinely want a job and that is why you are reading this book.

Try to make the best of your situation and overcome your barriers. Although it may be hard to find, look for that positive angle and concentrate on it.

How is Your Confidence ?

Have you ever noticed how people with bags of self confidence are always there in the thick of things, organising, directing, talking and enjoying their role. The world appears to be made up of extroverts and introverts with a few in between and it tends to be the extrovert, outgoing people who are seen as being the most successful. The nice guys and the quiet ones tend to be overlooked in the general rat race of life.

I am not a qualified psychologist, but I have been to 'the University of Life' and in the course of my own life experience I have observed people both professionally and socially. If you are really interested, there are dozens of books out there dealing solely with the subject of Self Confidence and extolling the power of positive thought. I tend to live in the real world and while I appreciate that a positive mental attitude is good, I do understand that we can't be upbeat all the time.

There has got to be a happy medium somewhere. A sort of half way house between the really pessimistic, miserable person and the person who is so bubbly and loud that they make you want to hit them!

What are you? Do you think 'the glass is half full', or 'the glass is half empty'? I once had a pessimistic friend who thought that 'the light at the end of the tunnel' was the headlights of a train coming the other way! When I said, 'cheer up' his reply was….. 'It's hard to smell the roses when you are up to your backside in weeds!' When I spoke to him at length, it turned out that he had quite serious money problems and a dodgy marriage. You can't just say 'cheer up, it may never happen', you are likely to get a smack in the mouth!

Some people have to sort out their personal situation before the positive thoughts come into play.

We must not of course assume that the quiet ones are necessarily pessimistic. The quiet ones in many cases just get on with the job and do it well without making a whole 'song and dance' about it.

Sometimes the extrovert ones are loud and brash to cover up some personal complex or shortcoming.

In the job hunting stakes, it tends to be the more self confident and extrovert people who manage to secure an interview and present themselves well. Of course not all companies want a person who is over confident and loud. Sometimes an interviewer may feel that their own job could be at risk from some brash know it all. On the other hand, an interviewer should not have to drag the answers out of the person they are interviewing. As we saw in the interview section, don't give 'yes'- 'no' answers.

If you are a naturally quiet introverted person, it's unlikely that you will change much in your adult life. People with loads of self confidence appear to be born that way. We all know of actors and singers who can go on to a stage and perform in front of hundreds of people. These folk are inspired to do even better by a positive reaction from the audience. There are of course others who don't even like small groups. If you find yourself at a social gathering, say at a party or in the pub, it won't take you long to see the self confident ones and those who prefer to stay in the background and listen.

One thing that I have to make clear is that the extrovert or self confident person is no better than the quiet one who may not feel so comfortable among others. Having said that, in the interview stakes, we must remember that 'first impressions last' and you will not make too good an impression if you come across as a 'little mouse' or a 'shrinking violet'.

Having confidence does not necessarily mean you have to be loud and brash. Just like doing a school exam, if you have done the study and you know your subject, then you should be able to convince an interviewer that you can do the job.

Obviously, there are specific jobs which do require an extrovert and confident personality. These are mainly customer facing roles, like Sales and Customer Service.

You must also understand that many roles do not require you to present a self confident image.

At the interview, you have to second guess what the interviewer is looking for. Many shy people, who get nervous at the thought of an interview, find a hidden self confidence when actually being interviewed.

Most people warm to a friendly outgoing personality as opposed to someone who is too serious.

There is no magic answer to 'Confidence building'. You can't take a pill and come out brimming with confidence ready to take on the world. The quieter ones, who may lack the ability to talk confidently at an interview, should try to play on their strengths. We all have an inner power that motivates and drives us to be successful in life. It's there; you have just got to find it. In the interview game, there is no substitute for knowing your subject and knowing about the job you are going for. Even the extrovert who thinks they can talk or bluff their way through, will not succeed unless the interviewer is convinced they actually know what they are talking about.

As we discussed previously, confidence can be enhanced by both your manners and dress style at the interview. You need to project a positive self image. Sometimes this can be hard if you have low self esteem. Perhaps you get upset by seeing people who are younger, taller, slimmer or better looking than yourself. In relation to the job hunting situation, you should appreciate that a potential employer is simply looking for someone who can do the job and fit in. You may only see the 'perfect people', but open your eyes. The majority are normal average folk getting on with their life. If someone does not like you for what ever reason, then that's their problem, not yours.

Confidence in relation to job hunting and attending interviews, comes from several things. The more interviews you attend the more confident you will become. Remember, the interviewer is only doing his or her job. The interviewer is not out to fail you or make you feel bad. They are simply looking for the person most suited to the position.

If your self confidence is not so good and you are a bit worried about the interview, remember, you actually managed to secure an interview where others did not! You must have 'something'. Go along with an open mind. Listen to the interviewer's questions. Think before you answer and have a few questions to ask back. Try to expand on your answers. Draw on that inner self confidence that *we all* have deep down. Go into the interview well prepared with a high 'got to' factor. Adopt a 'can do' attitude. Don't think 'oh, I've no chance. I bet the others will be better'. They may not be. This could be the job for you.

The Americans appear to have this 'positive attitude' off to a tee. I spent some time in the USA and came across many people in the service industry who said corny things like 'have a nice day'. The thing is, what ever way they said it; it always came across in a genuine and sincere way. These people in the public eye, like restaurant staff, shop people and petrol station staff may have left a disastrous situation at home, but they 'left it behind' and became professionals in the workplace.

I know you can't brush serious personal problems under the carpet, but don't bring them to the interview with you.

Remember, if you are one of the quiet ones who may not feel so comfortable in a person to person situation, just remind yourself that.... your job is to get a job. *You won't get a second chance to make a first impression.* Look at yourself in the mirror when you leave home. Ask, 'would I employ this person?' Create a positive self image and answer 'yes' to the question. You are unique and have special skills that only you have. Use these skills to present yourself in a positive light.

There is no harm in practicing your interview technique on your own at home. You may even like to involve a friend or member of the family to act as the interviewer. The more you practice, the more confident you should become. Make that extra special effort for the interview.

You may feel that I don't need to address the confident self assured people. Well I do. The confident ones may in some circumstances perform better at an interview than others, but these people should not become arrogant or assume they are naturally better than anyone else. I have interviewed many people in the course of my career and like many interviewers, can almost feel intimidated by someone who is loud and overbearing. Sometimes the loud and extrovert ones are hiding something and trying to cover the fact with 'bluster'.

To the talkers and the extroverts, I say, remember to listen to the interviewer and don't ramble on too much with 'flowery' answers.

If you do suffer from a slight lack of confidence, then your 'interview nerves' may be somewhat worse, but remember, if you don't enter the interview with a little apprehension then you will fail by being over confident!

In conclusion, I do not have a 'secret formula' to give you self confidence, but I do know that everyone has something special to offer the workplace. Do your research. Know what is required. 'Sell' yourself and remember, an interviewer is no better a person than you. If they are professional, they should make you feel at ease.

If you don't get the job it will obviously be a disappointment, but it's not the end of the world. You will be better prepared and more confident at the next interview. Put it behind you and concentrate on the next application.

A positive attitude is great, but it's still ok to feel 'down' now and again. Just don't wallow in gloom or self pity for too long. You will quickly realise that you are not going to win the lottery, so you have no alternative but to keep looking for work. This has to be done whether you have a confident personality or not. Adopt a 'can do' attitude and the rest should follow. It's a 'numbers game'. Know you will succeed. Be positive. Prepare properly and avoid setting yourself up for failure.

Visualise yourself as being successful and you stand a much better chance of achieving your goal and getting that good job.

How Resilient are You?

As we come to the end of our book, here is a little exercise which is both fun and serious.

I'd like you to think of what the word _Resilience_ means.

The dictionary describes it as 'recovering quickly from shock'.

Resilience is really wonderful. Resilient people appear to overcome setbacks that would make others give up.

Part of being resilient is being aware of stress and the things that cause stress......then doing something about it.

The person who is resilient has the ability to remain calm in situations of stress or pressure. They appear to be able to keep their emotions under control.

If you are out of work, or have money problems, then it is bound to be stressful.

Resilience can be divided into two types:

Emotional Resilience. This means not letting our emotions get the better of us. We are able to remain in full control of the situation. Emotional resilience involves the use of positive mental thought.

Just imagine we have batteries inside us. We know a battery has a limited life and once it's used up, it won't work any more. How do we 'recharge' our batteries? How much energy do we need? Where does the energy come from? How do we generate more energy?

Perhaps we take it for granted that the energy will always be there.

Emotional Resilience relies on the power of your inner strength. You have the ability to alter how you see a situation.

We all experience situations which affect us in either a good or bad way. We need to know what things 'drain our batteries' and what is needed to 'recharge' them again.

Proactive Resilience: Simply making the best of a bad situation and taking back control.

The exercise on the next page may help you 'recharge your batteries'.

'Recharging your Batteries'

Try this simple exercise:

Write down in the left hand column on the next page, the things that **'Drain your Batteries'**

That is, things which make you feel –
Low, sad, miserable, unhappy, stressed etc.

In the right hand column, write the things that **'Recharge your Batteries.'**

That is, things which make you –
Feel good, relieve stress, cheer you up etc.

NB If you don't want to write in the book, make your own list from page 102.

THINGS THAT DRAIN YOUR BATTERIES	THINGS THAT RE-CHARGE YOUR BATTERIES
-----------------------------	-----------------------------
-----------------------------	-----------------------------
-----------------------------	-----------------------------
-----------------------------	-----------------------------
-----------------------------	-----------------------------
-----------------------------	-----------------------------
-----------------------------	-----------------------------
-----------------------------	-----------------------------
-----------------------------	-----------------------------

You should see that even when your mind is filled with doom and gloom, you can still think of a few good and hopeful possibilities. When you are 'down', the positive angle may be hard to see, but it is there somewhere. Once you start on the list, it's amazing how you can see that things are not that bad.

For every negative, there should be a positive. You've just got to find it!

The Last Bit.

That's it. You have finished the book. By virtue of the fact that you have taken the trouble to read this information, you are already well ahead in the job search stakes. You now know more than you did before and more than anyone who has not read it at all.

Some of the information may have appeared a little obvious, but when added together, it's all important in preparing you for the job search task.

Remember, most of your activities involve trying to get an interview. Once you get the interview, then it's up to you to 'sell yourself' to the interviewer. Do the research on the job and company so as to be seen in the best possible light and be able to talk with confidence.

As I said before, 'looking for a job is a full time job in itself'. It's time consuming and frustrating. It's hard to remain positive when getting rejection after rejection, but many people are in the same situation. It is only those who keep at it, no matter what setbacks, will eventually succeed.

If you get fed up and a bit negative, then take a break from it all. We are all human and can't be positive all the time. I will say though, don't make that break too long. If you get too 'down' and start to take your 'eye off the ball', then it's a long climb back to a positive frame of mind.

I guess it is stating the obvious, to say that 99% of us work for money. We work to live, not live to work. That's OK. There is no harm in that. Having said that, it may be worth while thinking of a few other good reasons to work and have a job:-

- You will meet new friends.
- You will get out of the house.
- You will improve your self esteem.
- You should get useful training.
- You will gain more confidence.
- You will enjoy more peace of mind.
- Daytime television is awful !

I'm sure you can think of a few other good reasons. The money is of course, probably the most important. You can buy things you previously couldn't afford. You can go on holiday, pay your debts, go out more often, get a few luxuries and yes, even save a bit.

One final point I'd like to mention is the real need today to prove your qualifications with that vital certificate. There was a time when you could get away with a certain amount of 'flannel' on your CV, selling your experience and enthusiasm. These days, you need the 'bit of paper' to show you are qualified to the required standard.

Employers now issue a 'Job Profile' or 'Person Specification' outlining the qualifications and standards needed. No matter how long you have been in the job, or how experienced you are, employers need to see the certificate to show your competence.

This may mean that people who have not been involved in any study or courses for ages, now need to engage in training or attend college. This may not be a very cheerful prospect, but believe me when I say that you need to look into this seriously, sooner rather than later.

If you are out of work, this might be an ideal time to take on a course. If you are in work, look into NVQ's. The NVQ is a somewhat easier concept to grasp in that it is an assessment of you ability to do your existing job, as opposed to being academic or study based. There is a strong government and employer emphasis on having the correct qualifications. Check with the relevant college, or employer, or *Job Centre*. There is help out there for those people who are forward thinking enough to get their necessary certificates and be ahead of the rest.

When applying for jobs, you need to use every weapon in you armoury. The certificate, or licence or formal qualification will be of vital assistance in securing you the interview and hopefully the job.

Everything written here comes from personal experience. Although I am a teacher and trainer, I am not some high minded academic who doesn't live in the real world. I have known unemployment and financial difficulties. I've had to lower my sights and I have felt like giving up, but I didn't.

This book is geared to help you get a job, so please stick at it. Remember, it's use is not finished when you have read the last few words. It is a *reference book*. Keep it and refer to it when you need to upgrade your CV, or fill in an application form, or write a letter, or attend an interview.

Thank you for taking time to read 'The Postman is Late Again'. Let's hope you get some good news in the post soon.

Oh by the way, I didn't get a speeding ticket, but I did get a job - Result!

The End

Glossary of Terms

Agencies: Job Agencies/Recruitment Consultants. Companies that specialise in helping you find work. Some agencies cover specific types of work. Agencies should not charge you for their services.

Application Form: A document provided by a potential employer to be filled in by the applicant, detailing personal information, job history and suitability for the job.

Apprenticeship: Sometimes called 'Modern' Apprenticeship. This is the terminology which refers to a person learning a trade or skill, generally within a working environment or college.

Bullet Points:	Dots on a page, taken from your computer's tool bar to highlight specific points.
Block Capitals:	A general request when filling in an Application Form. Use Capitals (upper case) when writing.
Closing Date:	The date when the final applications will be accepted.
Contract:	In relation to employment, this is a document agreed upon between the Employer and Employee. It covers such things as:- The job description, the wages/salary, conditions of employment, rules and regulations, holidays, disciplinary procedure, termination of employment, health & safety and a few other things. The Contract should be signed by both the employer and employee.
CV:	Curriculum Vitae or Resume. A document prepared by yourself detailing personal information, work history and a personal profile. 'Functional' CV:- A general CV able to be presented to different employers. 'Targeted' CV:- A CV prepared with a specific job or company in mind.

Covering Letter: A letter sent to a specific employer who has advertised a vacancy. Generally sent with a CV.

CRB Check: 'Criminal Record Bureau'. A personal check carried out on anyone working with children or vulnerable persons.

ESOL: 'English for Speakers of Other Languages'. If English is not your native tongue and you need English language lessons, check out ESOL classes at your local college.

F E College: 'Further Education College'. Check out the courses to improve your skills or qualifications.

Health & Safety: A very important aspect of the modern working environment. A 'big thing' with all employers today. You must understand and obey the Health & Safety guidelines.

H R:
'Human Resources'. Used to be called The Personnel Department. Generally deals with all the employees in an organisation.

Jargon: Terminologies relating to a specific type of work or process. It is not nonsense, but shouldn't be used out of context.

Interviewee: The person being interviewed.

Interview Panel: This is where you are interviewed by more than one person. They are normally seated together in front of you. They may represent different departments within the company and could be male or female.

Job / Work History: In this context, it relates to the previous jobs you have had. These details are filled in on your CV and Application Form.

Networking: Asking around to check on job vacancies. Checking with your friends and family regarding possible vacancies.

Notice: To 'hand in your notice' or to 'be on your notice'. This refers to the time you must work before finishing your current job. This may be a contractual agreement. You may give, or be given, 'one week's' or 'one month's notice.'

NVQ: National Vocational Qualification. This is a Work Based qualification, designed to measure competence in a work related or professional role.

Personal Profile: Your own written profile, outlining your background, attributes and any other 'selling' points.

Professional:	Can be used to describe people in certain 'Professions' but also relates to the way we conduct ourselves in the workplace.
Pro Rata:	A Latin term generally quoted in relation to wages/salary and meaning that the rate of pay relates to the number of hours worked. A job ad. might have a 'full time' salary quoted with 'pro rata' written after it. Your income will be based on the full amount divided by the hours worked.
Redundancy:	Loss of your job through company problems or re-organisation. Nothing to be ashamed of.Remember, it's the job that was made redundant, not you.
Referees:	The people who give you a reference. Don't forget to ask them first!
The Package:	The Salary / Wages and other benefits you may get from an employer as an overall condition of employment.
Skills for Life:	The general term relating to Literacy and Numeracy ability. If you have difficulty with your reading, writing or math's, check local colleges for Literacy, Numeracy or ESOL courses.

Speculative Letter: A letter sent out on 'spec.' to potential employers who may have a vacancy but who have not actually advertised a position.

'Team Player': An employee or potential employee who can work well within a team or group of other workers.

'Temp': Short for Temporary, meaning that the job is not permanent. A person could be a 'temp' meaning that they do not work on a permanent basis. ie. covering for sick or maternity leave, or filling a 'short term' gap.

'Think outside the box': A term used to explain how someone should think beyond what is obvious. Come up with new ideas. Sometimes called: 'Thinking outside the square'.

Transferable Skills: Skills which you can bring to a new job that you have learnt or used in previous employment or experience.

A 'Week in hand': This terminology relates mostly to people who are paid weekly. It is a system where you are paid a week in arrears. In other words, you are not paid at the end of your first week's work. You are paid at the end of your second week's work, for your first week. This 'missed' first week will be paid when you finish your employment with the company. This system only applies to certain types of job and employer.

Work Based Learning: Learning centered on college or higher education, conducted in the actual workplace, allowing work experience to be tied in with education / learning.

Index

About the Author

Howard Coates lives in Hampshire. He comes from a Sales and Marketing background but has recently been involved in Training and Further Education. His subject speciality is in teaching the skills required to look for work and prepare for interview. He has helped many job seekers with these skills, from long term unemployed people to university graduates. The author has himself experienced redundancy and unemployment, so he certainly knows what he is talking about. The book is written in a professional but light hearted way, reflecting the author's general life experience.

www.ingramcontent.com/pod-product-compliance
Lightning Source LLC
Chambersburg PA
CBHW022007170526
45157CB00003B/1182